NOVIO BOY

NO QUIZ

THE EXCHANGE

Do people's opinions affect how we act? Why?

NOVIO BOY

A play

gary soto

 HAMPTON-BROWN

Hampton-Brown
P.O. Box 223220
Carmel, California 93922
800-333-3510
www.hampton-brown.com

Printed in the United States of America

ISBN-13: 978-0-7362-3153-4
ISBN-10: 0-7362-3153-6

06 07 08 09 10 11 12 13 14 15 10 9 8 7 6 5 4 3 2 1

ACKNOWLEDGMENTS

The playwright wishes to thank Arvin, El Centro, Garfield, Milby, Paramount, San Joaquin Memorial, and Sanger High Schools, which first mounted this play. He thanks Richard Talavera, who directed *Novio Boy* in its Bay Area premiere at the East Bay Center for the Performing Arts in March 1996.

THIS BOOK IS FOR CULTURE CLASH—
Herb Sigüenza, Richard Montoya, and
Ric Salinas—three funny *vatos*.

CONTENTS

INTRODUCTION

Gary Soto finished writing *Novio Boy* in 1996. It was his first play. The play is about a boy who seeks advice from his friends and family about his first date. Gary Soto was excited to see his play performed for the first time. He drove about 200 miles to watch the first production. For many years, he had written novels and poetry. Now his **drama** was finally appearing on a stage.

A play is a form of writing. The parts of a play are *acts* and *scenes*. A play often has two or more acts. An act is made of a group of scenes that tell a story. Actors usually perform plays for a live **audience** in a theater. The actors memorize their lines. They practice until they can perform the play in a natural way.

Key Concepts

drama *n.* stories written for performance on the stage

audience *n.* group of people who watch a performance

People who write plays are called *playwrights*. Playwrights create the play's characters, settings, and stories. They develop relationships between the characters. They tell the story by writing dialogue and physical actions for the characters. Playwrights provide directions in their plays to help actors perform each scene.

Novio Boy is a comedy. Gary Soto included certain comedic elements, like physical comedy, to make the play humorous. A comedy always has a happy ending. It amuses the audience with jokes. It is fun to watch.

Comedic Elements

Element	Definition
mistaken identity	a character (often in disguise) believed to be someone they are not
physical comedy	a type of comedy that relies on action to show humor
word play	finding humor in a word's sound or definition

Misunderstandings and coincidences are important elements of comedy. The audience understands the problems perfectly, but the characters are confused. The

Key Concepts

relationship *n.* connection between two or more people

comedy *n.* work of art that is meant to be funny

coincidence *n.* events that happen at the same time by accident audience laughs as the characters slowly realize what is happening.

Novio Boy explores young love through humor. Gary Soto created characters and situations that are both honest and funny. The play explores how Rudy's family and friends encourage or discourage him as he prepares for his first date. Everyone has an opinion: Rudy's mother, uncle, best friend, and even a complete stranger! Will he let their opinions affect him? Or will he listen to his own heart in his search for love?

PERFORMANCE NOTES

1. With the initial scene, players should let the lights come up and allow the audience to absorb the scene. Players should not rush into the dialogue, a tendency witnessed in many performances. This also applies to the openings of all other scenes.
2. Music used must be uncopyrighted, either original or in the public domain. The director should not "borrow" from popular songs.
3. The play takes place in Fresno, California, but references to towns, schools, restaurants, famous people, etc., may be changed for local appeal.
4. In scene 3, Uncle Juan's song should be sung with a country-western twang, employing, most likely, G, A, and D chords.
5. In scene 4, *"Tort y Frijoles"* should be sung with either a rap- or *ranchera*-like beat. The director must decide on the "sound."
6. In scene 5, Estela's wig (to accomplish change of hair color) could be hidden inside the hair dryer.

CHARACTERS

Rudy *ninth grader, small, sweet, funny*
Alex *ninth grader, big, awkward but wiser*
Patricia *eleventh grader, tall, romantic*
Alicia *eleventh grader, dry-humored* chola
Rudy's Mother *mid-thirties, attractive, and perky*
Uncle Juan *a Chicano loafer; looks like a hippie*
El Gato *a disc jockey*
Mama Rosa curandera *of love*
Estela *woman in beauty parlor*
Callers (6) *to radio show*
Old Man *crusty, but a good guy*
Waiter *quick and efficient*

SCENE ONE

*The scene begins in a backyard where two boys, both Mexican American, are philosophizing about girls. They are sloppy-looking, with holes in the knees of their pants. Stage right, **two girls are silhouetted** on a couch in a living room. The room is dim. Lights come up on RUDY and ALEX. RUDY **paces** back and forth and ALEX tries to keep up with him. RUDY throws himself down on a lawn chair. ALEX keeps pacing for a moment and then, noticing that his friend has sat down, joins him.*

RUDY: What am I gonna talk about? She's older than me and good-looking.

ALEX: Just level with her. Tell her you're sorry you look like you do.

RUDY: Sorry? You mean I should be sorry that I look like Tom Cruise? *(pause)* **You're cold, homes.** You're no help at all.

....

two girls are silhouetted *the shapes of two girls are seen*
paces *walks*
Just level with her. Just tell her the truth.
You're cold, homes. You are mean, friend.

15

ALEX: *(giggling)* Just joking, Rudy. Listen, man, you got to start simple. **Break the ice.** Ask her . . . what her favorite color is or something.

RUDY: Color?

ALEX: Yeah, color. Like, red or white.

RUDY: You mean, like, blue or yellow?

ALEX: Lavender!

RUDY: Purple!

ALEX: Forest green!

RUDY: Chevy **chrome**!

ALEX: That's it, man.

(RUDY gets up and starts to pace. ALEX gets up, too.)

RUDY: *(incredulous)* Colors?

ALEX: Colors. I picked up this little *secreto* from Mama Rosa on the Spanish **station**.

RUDY: Mama Rosa! You get your advice from her?

....

Break the ice. Just start the conversation.
chrome silver
(incredulous) *(doubtful)*
station radio station

ALEX: She's **for real**. She's an expert about love and things. She says you got to get your *boca* rattling. One thing leads to the next, you know.

RUDY: No, I don't know.

ALEX: Listen, man. Sometimes I'm talking about nothing and the next thing I know people are listening. Like I'm the president or something.

RUDY: You're not the president.

ALEX: I know that. What I'm saying is that you got to just talk stuff—anything!

*(Pause. RUDY **reflects**.)*

RUDY: I just start talking?

ALEX: That's right.

RUDY: Just . . . say things?

ALEX: Colors, start with colors. Just ask, "Patricia, what's your favorite color?"

RUDY: She won't think I'm weird?

....

for real serious
reflects *stops to think*

ALEX: No. She'll know immediately you're trying to start something, so she'll **play along**. She'll say something like "Green" or "Pink."

RUDY: And I'll tell her that my favorite color is dark blue.

ALEX: **There you go**, homes. *(pause)* So guess mine.

RUDY: Your what?

ALEX: My favorite color!

RUDY: Black and silver, like the Raiders?

ALEX: Nope.

RUDY: Blue and gold, like the Chargers?

ALEX: **Nah.** It's red, like my tongue.

(ALEX wiggles tongue at RUDY.)

RUDY: *(punching ALEX)* That's *asco!*

ALEX: *(chuckling)* Don't worry, homes. Just be **cool**.

RUDY: Cool.

ALEX: Like an iceberg.

....

play along answer your questions
There you go You understand
Nah. No.
cool calm

(The boys pace around the stage. They stop.)

RUDY: Man, I can't believe I'm **going out** with a girl in the eleventh grade. And yesterday, guess what I was doing.

ALEX: Helping your dad pour cement at a job site?

(RUDY shakes his head.)

ALEX: Lifting weights?

RUDY: You won't laugh if I tell you?

ALEX: Laugh at my best friend?

RUDY: *(hesitates; long pause)* I was playing **G.I. Joes** with my cousin Isaac. Man, it was fun. G.I. Joe was beating up Ken, and Barbie was kicking back watching the *pleitos*.

(ALEX laughs.)

RUDY: I got another problem. I told Patricia I was taking her to **grub** at Steaks, Steaks, y Más Steaks.

ALEX: You told her you were taking her there? What's wrong with you, homes? Those hamburgers cost twice as much as McDonald's. And you got to **tip**, too.

(RUDY reflects on his error.)

....

going out going on a date
G.I. Joes with action figures; with dolls
grub eat
tip pay extra money for good service

ALEX: You got enough money?

RUDY: How much do you think I'll need?

ALEX: At least fifteen bones.

RUDY: Fifteen dollars!

(RUDY shakes his head and shrugs his shoulders. ALEX starts to go through his pockets.)

ALEX: *(teasing)* Here, this should help.

(RUDY takes ALEX's quarter and looks at it.)

RUDY: *(sarcastically)* You're cool, Alex. This quarter might get me a piece of gum.

*(They sit and reflect on the **dilemma**.)*

ALEX: *(perks up)* Let me give you some advice. You got to talk intelligent, like you know something.

RUDY: Like I know something?

ALEX: Remember, she's two years ahead of you and in eleventh grade. You got to be ***suave***, kind of like—*pues*, like me. *(hooks a thumb at himself)*

....

(sarcastically) *(jokingly)*
dilemma *problem*
(perks up) *(gets more excited)*
suave *polite, charming*

RUDY: Help me then, Alex.

ALEX: *(thinking about it)* **It so happens I got this** love letter from Sylvia Hernandez. Remember her?

RUDY: No.

ALEX: Yeah, you do. She threw up *huevos con* **weenies** in fifth grade. *(imitates someone vomiting)* It was all over the classroom and down the hall. It was like that old movie *The Blob* after she was all done.

RUDY: *(reflecting)* Yeah, I remember that girl now. She got some on my shoes. *(pause)* So what did the letter say?

ALEX: *(reaches into his pocket)* Got it right here.

(ALEX sniffs the letter for perfume, and RUDY sniffs it as well. ALEX starts to read letter.)

ALEX: "Alex, I think you have the coolest eyes. And the cutest nose."

RUDY: You got a fat *huango* nose.

ALEX: Hey, **dude**, you want me to help you or not?

RUDY: **I take that back.** You got a real cute nose. *(pulls up his own nose into the shape of a pig's snout)*

....

It so happens I got this I received a
weenies hot dogs
dude man, friend
I take that back. I did not mean what I said.

ALEX: That's better. *(continues reading)* "I really care about you a lot, Alex. I really don't know how to say this, but here goes. I think that you like me but don't want to tell me because of what your friends might say. Forget them. They don't have to live your life. You do! Last year I fell totally in love with this guy Kendall—"

RUDY: What kind of name is Kendall?

*(ALEX **gives RUDY a look**.)*

ALEX: *(continues reading)* "At first Kendall was nice to me. Then he started being mean to me and **talking behind my back**. It hurt me when he told this girl from Selma that I **was stuck-up**. I guess it was to get me to stop liking him. But I didn't stop liking him for a long time. Now I like you, Alex. I dream about—"

RUDY: Man, she knows how to talk.

ALEX: ¡*Cállate!* You're interrupting the flow of my love letter. *(pause)* Here's a good part. "Alex, you're nicer than Kendall. You're cute, too. All the boys from Roosevelt are cute, but you're the cutest. Please don't be like Kendall. I will **shower you with kisses** forever and ever."

RUDY: *(takes the letter and examines it)* Sounds like poetry. No, like *mi abuelita's telenovelas*.

....

gives RUDY a look *looks meanly at RUDY*
talking behind my back *saying mean things about me*
was stuck-up *thought I was better than everyone*
shower you with kisses *give you many kisses*

ALEX: This letter should be the **floor plan** for your love life. You got to **lay it on thick**. Be romantic, *ese*. *Suave*.

RUDY: *(reflecting)* Suave. *(pulls out a small notepad)* I better write some of this stuff down so I don't forget: "Be romantic." "Lay it on thick."

ALEX: I went on a date once.

RUDY: You're lying.

ALEX: No, I did. *(pause)* It wasn't exactly a date. Me and this girl went to the playground.

RUDY: Get serious.

ALEX: Yeah, I picked her up on my bike and . . . don't laugh.

RUDY: Why would I laugh at my best friend?

ALEX: I can see it. You're gonna laugh!

RUDY: No, I promise.

*(RUDY and ALEX **trade glances**.)*

ALEX: She had to pedal the bike because I didn't have enough leg strength. It's hard with two people!

....

floor plan example you follow
lay it on thick be extra nice to her
trade glances *look at each other quickly*

*(RUDY chokes, **muffling** his laugh.)*

ALEX: *(continuing)* It was a lot of fun. We spent a couple hours on the **monkey bars**. Then we played tetherball, and then a game of chess. Yeah, it was going pretty good—until Frankie Torres came by and started teasing me.

RUDY: Frankie did that?

ALEX: Yeah. Because I was **all dressed up**. *(laughs)* I had on this pink shirt, and a bow tie, and **buckets of my dad's Aqua Velva**.

RUDY: Dressed up at the playground?

ALEX: Yeah, plus . . .

RUDY: What?

(ALEX kicks at the ground, embarrassed.)

RUDY: Hey, I'm your *carnal*.

ALEX: She was getting a drink of water, so I was holding her purse.

RUDY: And that's when Frankie saw you.

ALEX: *(nodding his head)* He called me a girl because I had her

....

muffling trying to hide the sound of
monkey bars playground equipment
all dressed up wearing nice clothes
buckets of my dad's Aqua Velva too much cologne

purse on my shoulder. *(Pause. ALEX stands up.)* That was my first date. Age nine.

*(RUDY shakes his head **sympathetically**. He takes the letter from ALEX and reads it silently. **Lights fade.**)*

....

sympathetically understandingly; with care
Lights fade. The lights go dim, and the scene ends.

SCENE TWO

*Lights **come up** on PATRICIA and ALICIA, sitting on a couch with a magazine. They're playing the game of choosing the best-looking guy on the page.*

PATRICIA: I got this one.

ALICIA: I got this one.

PATRICIA: This gorgeous face.

ALICIA: This hot tamale.

PATRICIA: This enchilada.

ALICIA: That soft taco.

PATRICIA: Umm . . . this one.

.

....

come up *shine*

This gorgeous face. This handsome face is the best-looking one on the page.

ALICIA: *(pouting)* I wanted that one! His hair is so cute! *(tosses magazine aside)*

PATRICIA: My brother, Eddie, and I used to pick toys like this. Me and my brother would go through the Toys "R" Us ads and—

ALICIA: —and pick the best toys. We played that, too.

PATRICIA: Now we're picking boys.

ALICIA: Toys or boys, it's all the same.

*(The girls **give each other high fives**; they get up from couch.)*

ALICIA: Now you got this **hot date**.

PATRICIA: Rudy's really sweet. He's got these little dimples and hair that bounces when he walks.

ALICIA: Girl, you're lucky. Dimples are so cute!

PATRICIA: And long eyelashes.

ALICIA: *(shivering)* Dimples and eyelashes.

PATRICIA: And get this. He's taking me to Steaks, Steaks, y Más Steaks!

....

(pouting) (looking sad)
give each other high fives slap hands to show happiness
hot date really exciting date
And get this. And listen to this information.

ALICIA: No, girl.

PATRICIA: Cross my heart.

ALICIA: *(shaking her head)* You're lucky, Pat. You get a hamburger, and you get to fall in love, too.

PATRICIA: And he's extra nice to me when he's serving in the cafeteria. He really plops on those chili beans.

ALICIA: You mean that *escuincle* in the cafeteria? Isn't he just in ninth grade?

PATRICIA: So?

ALICIA: What do you mean, "So"? **You're robbing the cradle.** He's a ninth grader. He's probably still carrying his Power Ranger lunch box to school.

PATRICIA: He's only two grades behind. It's nothing, girl. These are modern times. It's OK to **date down**.

ALICIA: It doesn't bother you?

PATRICIA: No, not really.

ALICIA: I mean, he's, like, just out of his high chair.

PATRICIA: It's just a date. *(pause)* Life is really strange. Like,

----

Cross my heart. I promise I am telling the truth.

You're robbing the cradle. You are dating someone who is too young for you.

date down date people who are younger than you

we've been alive sixteen years, almost seventeen. We're not kids anymore. *(pause)* I can remember when I was playing with Barbie and Ken, and I was making Ken kiss Barbie really hard.

ALICIA: Ken was **hot stuff**, huh?

PATRICIA: But then I got my brother's G.I. Joe and had him **beat up** Ken. Kicked sand right in his face. *¡Híjole!* G.I. Joe kissed even harder. I thought they would have to get married.

ALICIA: Yeah, I remember my Barbie. My stupid brother tore her head off and used it for a baseball with his stupid friends.

PATRICIA: That's **sorry**.

ALICIA: **I got the dude back.** When my parents were gone one day, I threw him outside with only his *chones* on.

PATRICIA: No!

ALICIA: That's what he deserved. I made him stay out there on the porch.

PATRICIA: In his *chones?*

ALICIA: Dirty ones, too, all *fuchi y cochino.* Then the mail lady

....

hot stuff really attractive
beat up fight with
sorry stupid, sad
I got the dude back. I did something mean to him, too.

came and my brother didn't know what to do, except pick up the cat and try to hide himself.

(Pause. They look at a magazine.)

PATRICIA: I'm going to get my hair **done**.

ALICIA: Short and with bangs?

(PATRICIA shakes her head.)

ALICIA: Long, with a little wave?

(PATRICIA shakes her head again.)

PATRICIA: Curls.

ALICIA: Curls?

PATRICIA: Lots of curls. I'm going to get my hair done at the House of Beauty.

(ALICIA smiles. They turn the pages of the magazine.)

PATRICIA: Look at this one. He's good-looking.

ALICIA: Yeah, but my mom says don't trust any guy with green eyes. She says that men with green eyes can't be trusted.

....

done cut, styled

PATRICIA: *(clicking her tongue)* Parents are so **superstitious**.

ALICIA: **Old-fashioned.**

PATRICIA: Old, *old*-fashioned.

(They turn the pages of the magazine.)

ALICIA: *(perks up)* I got him.

PATRICIA: Him?

ALICIA: The guy behind him.

PATRICIA: This little cutie.

*(They smile at the **spread** of handsome young boys in the magazine, then toss it aside.)*

ALICIA: Remember when I burned my report card?

PATRICIA: *(searching her memory)* Your report card?

ALICIA: I got all those terrible grades and I knew my mom was gonna get mad at me. So I burned it on the front lawn and . . . *híjole*, I burned the whole front lawn.

PATRICIA: I remember. You tried to blame it on lightning.

....

superstitious worried about bad luck
Old-fashioned. Traditional.
spread pictures

ALICIA: That was stupid, huh? *(pause)* I guess we are growing up. We're in eleventh grade. Now when I get a bad report card, I just type in some good grades.

*(The girls sit on the couch, each **lost in her own thoughts**. There is the sound of a **low-rider car**. The girls get up and look out the front window, watching the car cruise down the street.)*

PATRICIA: That's a nice ride.

ALICIA: He's hitting the switch. *(calling to low-rider)* **Hop it**, brown boy! Hop it!

*(The girls' heads go up and down, watching the low-rider **employ its hydraulics**. The noise of the low-rider fades and the girls turn away from the window.)*

ALICIA: What are you going to wear on your date?

PATRICIA: *(reflecting)* Maybe my jeans and a white top. Keep it simple . . . Think I should help pay for lunch?

ALICIA: *Pues,* he invited you, *qué no?* Just leave the tip. That'll show you care about him.

PATRICIA: How do you know all this?

ALICIA: I read it in *Low-Rider.* They had a special on how to get guys to like you.

....

lost in her own thoughts thinking
low-rider car car that is close to the ground
Hop it Make the car bounce
employ its hydraulics bounce

*(Music slowly rises. The girls freeze as lights come up on the other side of the stage to reveal El Gato, the suave Chicano **disc jockey**.)*

EL GATO: We're coming to you *raza* with **heavy hitmakers** from the sixties . . . It's dedication time . . .

(A portion of a song plays.)

EL GATO: *(continuing)* Time for some love notes from you **lovebirds**. Here's one from Smiley to his girl in Dinuba . . . Here's one from Marta to her *novio,* Samuel. She says, "Let's get together when I get out of juvie." El Güero says to his little cookie, "Don't crumble 'cause I cheated on you." *Ay, este malo chavalo.* Let's forget that dude. And here's one from Jesús to his baby love in Fowler, and we got something from as far away as Tulare . . . Yeah, it's a *quinceañera* for Lupe de la Rosa. Way to go, girl. Fifteen and still pecking away at school, it says here. Here's a little *dedica* to Carolina from her secret admirer, who says, **"I only got eyes for you."** *(pause)* I'm El Gato and I'm coming to you *vivo, raza,* from K-Crudo . . .

(Lights fade on El Gato as the music fades. Lights on girls.)

ALICIA: El Gato is cool.

....

disc jockey radio announcer
heavy hitmakers popular singers
lovebirds people who are in love
"I only got eyes for you." "You are the only person I love."

PATRICIA: Why don't we **call him up**?

ALICIA: *Chale.* I'm too scared.

PATRICIA: What's there to be scared of?

ALICIA: I don't know. Just talking to someone who's on the radio.

(long pause as they look at magazines)

PATRICIA: Who's the most important person you've ever talked to?

ALICIA: What do you mean?

PATRICIA: You know, like a **movie star or a rocker**.

ALICIA: *(thinks for a moment)* Don't laugh.

PATRICIA: I won't.

ALICIA: I can see that you're gonna laugh.

PATRICIA: *¡En serio!* I promise.

ALICIA: *(shyly) Pues,* it was Ronald McDonald.

(PATRICIA laughs.)

....

call him up call him with the telephone
movie star or a rocker famous movie actor or a musician

ALICIA: See, I knew you were going to laugh. I don't care. So who did you meet that was so big and important? Ed Olmos? Carlos Santana? Jimmy Smits? Culture Clash?

PATRICIA: Well, he's **just a notch below them**.

ALICIA: Who, then?

PATRICIA: Promise you won't laugh? And if you do, I don't care.

(ALICIA crosses her heart.)

PATRICIA: Well, I met the San Diego Chicken.

ALICIA: The San Diego Chicken?

PATRICIA: You know, the chicken that's the **mascot** for the baseball team. The San Diego Padres.

ALICIA: The chicken? *¿El gallo?*

PATRICIA: I even got his **autograph**.

ALICIA: The dude's chicken scratch? *(laughs)* I didn't know chickens could hold a pen. *(pause)* We've never met anyone famous.

PATRICIA: I guess that's why we're scared to call El Gato.

....

just a notch below them not as famous as they are
mascot symbol, representative
autograph signature

ALICIA: What's there to worry about? *No te preocupes.* Let's call the *vato.* I want to hear "Ninety-six Tears." That's my favorite **oldie**.

PATRICIA: *Es mi favorito, también.* Hey, did you know that I cried exactly ninety-six tears when I **broke up with** Robert?

ALICIA: *Mentirosa.* You're lying, girl.

PATRICIA: Cross my heart, *flaca.* Ninety-six *lágrimas!*

*(PATRICIA and ALICIA **bury** their heads and pretend to cry. Music plays briefly. Song fades. Lights darken.)*

....

oldie old song
broke up with quit dating
bury cover

BEFORE YOU MOVE ON...

1. **Text Features** Reread pages 15–16. How do the stage directions help you understand the scene?

2. **Comparisons** Rudy and Patricia both talk to a friend about the date. How are their conversations similar?

LOOK AHEAD Read to page 58. How should Rudy act on his date?

SCENE THREE

*Lights come up on Rudy's MOTHER in the living room, lifting small weights. RUDY joins her **in a comical imitation**. After **a "rep"** she starts to jump rope and move around the stage comically. RUDY follows along. She drops on the floor and takes a **swig** from her squeeze bottle.*

MOTHER: Got to stay **in shape**, *m'ijo*.

RUDY: Mom, you're already in shape.

(MOTHER smiles at the compliment and starts to do sit-ups.)

RUDY: Mom, who was your first boyfriend?

MOTHER: I had only one boyfriend—your daddy.

RUDY: Mom, level with me. I was born fourteen years ago. I know a lot.

....

in a comical imitation *by imitating her in a funny way*
a "rep" *lifting the weights*
swig *quick drink*
in shape *healthy and strong*

(MOTHER stops her sit-up routine.)

MOTHER: *(laughs)* What do you know?

RUDY: You know! Things! Like about the **birds and the bees**, and the cats and the dogs, and the 'Niners and the Raiders.

MOTHER: *(dreamily)* *Pues,* I did have one boyfriend before your father.

RUDY: Really?

MOTHER: He was from Michoacán. He had beautiful green eyes and red boots made from lizard skin. He was a gentleman, not a *borracho.* He had a thin little mustache. He danced beautifully and read poetry to me in the park. *(snaps out of her dream)* *¿Por qué?* Why do you want to know these things?

RUDY: I have something to tell you.

MOTHER: Don't tell me! You lost your gym clothes again.

RUDY: No, it's worse—I mean, better. *(pause)* Mom, I'm going out with a girl tomorrow.

MOTHER: *¿Qué?*

....

birds and the bees relationships between men and women
(dreamily) (happily)
snaps out of quickly stops
Don't tell me! Let me guess what you are going to say.

RUDY: I told this girl that I would take her out for a hamburger. *(quickly)* Can I borrow fifteen **bucks**?

MOTHER: *¡Espérate! ¿Quién es esta muchacha?*

RUDY: Just a friend.

MOTHER: You're too little to have friends. *(realizes she sounds ridiculous) Pues,* a friend like that.

RUDY: **Come on, Mom.** Make it ten dollars, then.

MOTHER: You think money **grows on trees**? *(pause)* Who is this girl, anyway?

RUDY: Her name's Patricia Gomez. She's really, really, really, really, really cute. She's got this nose like this. *(pushes up his nose)* She's smart and even president of the Spanish Club. *(looks at audience, steps forward, and conjugates the verbs "to remember" and "to give")* Recuerdo, recuerdas, recuerda, recordamos, recordáis, y recuerdan; doy, das, da, damos, dais, y dan.

MOTHER: *¡Cállate!* **You sound like a broken record.**

RUDY: Yeah, she's really nice. But there's one problem, Mom.

MOTHER: *¡Qué!* What is it?

....

bucks dollars
Come on, Mom. Do not be silly, Mom.
grows on trees is easy to get; is free
You sound like a broken record. You are repeating yourself.

RUDY: She's older than me.

MOTHER: Older?

(RUDY nods his head.)

MOTHER: How much older?

RUDY: Well, you know, she's **an upperclassman** in high school.

*(MOTHER sits down, **shocked**. RUDY tries to comfort her.)*

RUDY: Mom, you got nice biceps.

MOTHER: **Never mind my muscles.** How come you can't find a girl your own age?

RUDY: They're all **taken**. *(pause)* Come on, Mom. You're a little older than Dad.

MOTHER: Just two years older than your *papi*. I look younger. That's what your *nina* says. Do you see any wrinkles on my face?

(RUDY takes his MOTHER's face between his hands and examines it.)

MOTHER: And my hair? *Mira.* Black as the night.

....

an upperclassman in one of the higher grades
shocked surprised
Never mind my muscles. My muscles are not important.
taken dating someone else

RUDY: Naturally black?

MOTHER: *Pues,* I did touch it up at the parlor. Just around my ears.

RUDY: Touch it up?

MOTHER: All right, I mean **dye**! Can you tell?

RUDY: *(sniffing)* **The chemicals.**

MOTHER: You can smell my hair? Come on!

(RUDY nods his head. MOTHER touches her hair.)

MOTHER: *(walks around the stage)* So now you have a girlfriend?

RUDY: Nah, Mom, not a girlfriend. A friend. And she's just two years older. *(pause)* Come on, Mom. I'll pay you back when I get a job.

MOTHER: Sure you will. You'll get married and move away and never think of your mommy.

RUDY: Mom, I'm just going out for a hamburger, not getting married.

MOTHER: Is she a nice girl?

....

dye change the color

The chemicals. I can smell the chemicals that are used to change hair color.

Sure you will. No, you will not.

RUDY: *Seguro que sí.*

MOTHER: *(reflects)* If you go on this date, I want you to be nice. *¿Entiendes?*

RUDY: Just like the dude you knew before you met Dad.

MOTHER: It's important that you act like a gentleman. Show some pride. Don't be a *mocoso.*

RUDY: Was Dad a gentleman when you were dating him?

MOTHER: *Claro que sí.* Strong and clever and full of ideas about getting rich in America. Your *papi* is a clever man, just like you, *m'ijo.*

RUDY: And dedicated.

MOTHER: *Muy fuerte y bravo.* In only two years he **got his own** cement truck. Who would have ever thought? *Jefe* of his own **crew.** *(pause)* This is a good country.

RUDY: What do you mean?

MOTHER: Your *papi* has a job and I have **my chair** at the beauty parlor. One day you'll be going to college. *(examines RUDY's hair)* I need to cut your hair . . . *(sniffs the air)* ¡Ay, los frijoles!*

....

got his own was promoted at work so that he has his own
crew team of workers
my chair my own special chair for customers to sit in so that
I can earn money

*(MOTHER runs from living room. RUDY starts lifting her weights. He does an **aerobics** routine comically and gets tired almost immediately. Enter UNCLE JUAN with his guitar.)*

JUAN: *(sniffs the air)* Ay, your mommy must be cookin' her regular *cosa* of burnt beans. *(pause)* Rudy-tudy. Bo-bo Bo-booty, banana, ramama-moody Rudy-tudy! *¿Qué pasa?*

RUDY: *(downcast)* Hey, Uncle.

JUAN: How come you making *jeta.*

RUDY: It's nothing.

JUAN: Nothing? What do you mean, nothing? Everything is something . . . Here, listen to my song that never **made the top one million**. *(He begins to play and sing with country-western twang)* No menudo en mi bowl y nada en mi estómago. Nothing in my wallet but a little crushed Lifesaver. *Nada, nada, nadaaaaaa!* . . . Now you see why it was never a **hit**. So what's the problem?

RUDY: I'm going out with a girl.

JUAN: That's a problem? For a minute, I thought you didn't make the soccer team.

RUDY: *Tío,* I don't have any money for my date.

....

aerobics *exercise*
(downcast) *(sad)*
made the top one million became famous
hit popular song

JUAN: *No problema,* Rudy!

RUDY: Uncle, you're **playing with** me.

JUAN: *En serio.* Money is the last thing you have to worry about when you go on a date. Worry about what you have to say, little Romeo.

RUDY: That's what Alex says. He says girls like it when you sound like you know something.

JUAN: Exactly. You got to move your *boca.* Whatever you do, don't get **heavy** on her or you'll scare her away.

RUDY: Break-the-ice kind of talk?

JUAN: ¡*Simón!* The first time I went with a girl, man, I **freaked her out**. I told her that I thought I had been captured by **a UFO**.

RUDY: No, you didn't!

JUAN: *Simón.* It was way back in the seventies. I told her about the UFO and this out-of-body experience. Freaked her out!

RUDY: Uncle, were you a hippie?

....

playing with teasing
heavy too serious
freaked her out scared her
a UFO aliens; a spaceship

JUAN: A Chicano hippie, *lo mejor,* the best. *(Gives a peace sign and shouts to audience)* Peace . . . love . . . *¡Viva la raza! (to RUDY)* Man, I was **a trip**. I had these **bad-looking bell bottoms** and a tie-dyed T-shirt. Love beads and a peace sign. I wore these groovy glasses. Far out, man, that's how I was. *(brings out a pair of John Lennon glasses, strums his guitar)*

(RUDY's head bobs to the music. MOTHER returns from the kitchen.)

JUAN: Hey, hey, here comes our **money tree** swaying real pretty. *(sweetly)* Hey, *hermana,* how are things? You looking tough.

MOTHER: *(stops for a second and **poses for** them)* You think so?

JUAN: Like a model for pots and pans at the Kmart on Kings Canyon. You do something with your hair?

(RUDY pulls his UNCLE away.)

RUDY: *(in near whisper)* Don't mention her hair.

JUAN: *(confused)* ¿Qué?

RUDY: She's dyeing it.

(JUAN nods his head.)

....

a trip funny
bad-looking bell bottoms great pants
money tree money giver; provider
poses for *shows her strong muscles to*

RUDY: Mom, Uncle's right. You're tough-looking.

JUAN: And dependable, like a five-year battery from Kragen's. *(pause)* Sis, can you lend me **a sweet twenty-five**? Be a *pan dulce*—sweet!

MOTHER: You think money grows on trees? First Rudy and now you! And you compare me to a cheap battery?

JUAN: I'm talkin' in metaphors. *(strums guitar to audience)* Soy un poeta de Aztlán. ¡Viva la raza! *(to sister)* Come on, *hermana.* How about *veinte dolares*?

*(MOTHER gives him a **stern** look, hands on hips.)*

JUAN: How about ten bucks and that bag of crushed aluminum cans on the back porch?

MOTHER: *(seriously)* Juan.

JUAN: ¿Qué, hermana?

MOTHER: You got to stop **your nonsense. It's about time you got** a regular job.

JUAN: One from eight to five?

MOTHER: No, a job from six in the morning to eight at night. To make up for lost time.

....

a sweet twenty-five twenty-five dollars
stern mean, serious
your nonsense being silly
It's about time you got You should get

JUAN: *¡Chale!* I can't work like that. What if my **bum** friends look up from the gutter and see me in a white shirt and a tie? Have you thought about that? **The peer pressure? The alienation? Cultural rejection?** Angst *y todo?*

MOTHER: *(softens)* Maybe some people aren't meant for regular jobs.

JUAN: That's me, *hermana.* *(pause)* And I'll pay you back. I got a part-time job.

MOTHER: You? Working?

JUAN: I got a job playing *guitarra.* *(pause)* The money's not for me. It's for Rudy. Come on, Sis, open up.

(MOTHER softens even more. She goes through her purse for money and hands it over to RUDY.)

MOTHER: It's a month early, but this is your birthday money.

RUDY: It's all clean, too. Thanks, Mom.

MOTHER: It went through the washer. It was in your *papi's* pants.

JUAN: *(bending over the ten-dollar bill)* I haven't seen a ten-dollar

....

bum lazy, jobless

The peer pressure? The alienation? Cultural rejection? The way my friends will act toward me? How I won't be their friend anymore? How they all will ignore me?

bill in ten years. I love the smell of money. *(sniffs burning frijoles)* And your cooking, *hermana*. Rudy, go **turn off the beans**.

*(RUDY runs **offstage**.)*

MOTHER: You really got a job?

JUAN: *¡Simón!* I got a job playing guitar at Steaks, Steaks, y Más Steaks. I start tomorrow.

MOTHER: That's good news, Juan. *(pause)* But, Juan, the seventies are over. You got to **get settled down**. *¿Entiendes?*

JUAN: Don't talk like that, sis. I just wanna play guitar. Bring *la música a la gente!* *(strums his guitar as he walks offstage.)*

(MOTHER sniffs her burning beans on the stove and runs offstage. Lights dim.)

....

turn off the beans turn off the stove

offstage *off the stage as if he is going to another room or another place*

get settled down become more responsible

SCENE FOUR

Lights come up on EL GATO. Slow-dance music.

EL GATO: We're coming to you, *raza,* from *el gran* station K-Crudo. We got a little romance happening in Orange Cove. It's Manuel and Manuela . . . Ay, the little brown M&M's . . . Got *una dedica* from Shirley to Louie, who's celebrating his driver's permit. **Way to go**, dude. We got some more *gente* on the road. Just be sure to stay between the lines . . . And now we got a special guest coming to you. It's the Doctor of Love, Mama Rosa, a *curandera* who works out of her garage with her **old man, a body-and-fender specialist**. If you want to contact her, you can call her sister-in-law at *uno, dos, tres—pues.*

ROSA: That's right, El Gato. People can call me *cuando quieran* at *uno, dos, tres—pues.*

....

Way to go Congratulations; Good job
old man, a body-and-fender specialist husband, a car repairperson

EL GATO: *(into microphone)* OK, *raza*, listen up. She's got a **special on broken hearts** this week. If you bring in your *coche*, you can get some Bondo work *también*. Think about it, *gente*. It's almost a two-for-one. You get to kick-start your love life and get a smooth-looking fender to boot. *(pause)* So, Rosa, how do opposites attract?

ROSA: By the shifting of stars and the moon lining up with Venus—

EL GATO: Check that out, *radiolandia*.

ROSA: —and the pull of the waves under a meteor shower.

EL GATO: That sounds pretty spacey, but can you give us some **tips**? Our listeners—and some of the lonely dudes *y chicas* in the audience—want to solve this problem of boy-meets-girl. So give it up, Mama Rosa. What's the secret?

ROSA: We're talking **love potions**, *qué no*?

EL GATO: You're the source, baby.

ROSA: I'll get to the potions soon enough. Let me start with the stare. *(stands up and, bug-eyed, slowly approaches audience)* If a young woman sees a young man staring at her while he's touching his nose, that means he likes her for the moment. But later, you watch, he's going to **thumb his nose at her**.

....

special on broken hearts sale for sad people
tips advice
love potions magical drinks that make people fall in love
thumb his nose at her be mean to her

EL GATO: That's cold. The old thumb-your-nose-at-your-ex-*vieja* trick.

ROSA: If a young woman is staring at a man while adjusting her purse strap, she wants money.

EL GATO: Is that so?

ROSA: *Sí, señor.* And if a man is staring at a woman while she's eating a burrito, it means that he just wants her to cook and clean for him. The *vato's* no good.

EL GATO: *¡Híjole!* This is valuable information, *gente.* So, if staring's no good, how can we get our people together in romance?

ROSA: Bingo.

EL GATO: *¿Qué?*

ROSA: *Sí,* bingo. Some of the nicest people in the world play bingo every week.

EL GATO: I thought you met nice people at church.

ROSA: No, El Gato, that's where the **sinners** go to make themselves feel better. Nice young people go to play bingo in the church basement. It's a lot of fun. You get a couple of cards, some coffee with Sweet 'N Low, maybe a

....

Is that so? I did not know that.
Bingo. A game called bingo.
sinners bad, guilty people

basket of popcorn, and it's a **beautiful atmosphere for discriminating people**. *Pues,* you get to hear *chisme.*

EL GATO: But tell us about those love potions.

ROSA: *Un momento.* I have something important to say to the young ladies out there. Advice, I mean. *(leans toward the audience)* It's the *huevo* test.

EL GATO: The *huevo* test?

ROSA: It's not what you think, *hombre. (pause)* Take a *huevo* and rub it on your old man's forehead when he's asleep and then cook it for him. If you crack the egg and some hair comes out, *pues,* it's a bad sign. *Muy malo.* Move out of town. Get back to Mexico if you have to.

EL GATO: *(fanning himself)* Ay, dios. I don't know if I like this *huevo* exam.

ROSA: *(makes faces at EL GATO) Pero* if you crack the egg and the yolk comes out pretty and clean-looking, it means that he's a good guy.

EL GATO: My *huevos* are **spanking** clean, *mujer.*

ROSA: Now, about potions. I recommend a simple one. Put three drops of lemon juice plus one or two of your tears

....

beautiful atmosphere for discriminating people great place
for people who want to date good people

(fanning himself) (acting nervous)

spanking very

in a glass of water. Place the glass under your *novio's* bed. In the morning, rush over to his house. If you discover that the water is **dingy**—*pues,* do I have to tell you he's no good?

EL GATO: *¡Chihuahua!*

ROSA: *De veras.* The water will turn all ugly. *Pero* if the water is clear, have your *novio* drink half of it, and you drink the other half. Then the magic happens. **You're no longer thirsty for** other people. **You're hooked.**

EL GATO: Like a fish?

ROSA: You got it. As I say, love **is eternal** . . . as long as it lasts.

EL GATO: Wow, Mama Rosa. I want to thank you for coming on my show. For all your troubles, I got a couple of tickets for you to see the wrestling match at the fairgrounds. *Buena suerte. Muchísimas gracias. (into the microphone)* That was *muy interesante.* Our next guest is that cool, *suave* cat, that number-one *guitarrista del valle* who has finally, finally, finally found a job. I mean, the dude is working. Give it up, *gente,* for the *vato* Juan-Juan.

(JUAN walks out from stage left, waving to the audience. He strums has guitar. He blows a kiss to the audience.)

....

dingy dirty
You're no longer thirsty for You do not want to date
You're hooked. You are in love.
is eternal goes on forever

EL GATO: How you doing, bro? Long time no see.

JUAN: Yeah, long time since I was on your show. What, two years?

EL GATO: I think you were playing *tu guitarra* on the street or at the **swap meet**, *qué no?*

JUAN: That's right, bro. I was taking the music to the people and collecting a little **chump change** for myself.

EL GATO: And now you got a job?

JUAN: Yeah, I'm playing over at Steaks, Steaks, y Más Steaks. I'm inviting everybody I don't owe money to to come over and hear me. I'm going to **silence the critics about** Chicano music. It's the best, *carnal. ¡Lo mejor!*

EL GATO: I like to hear that. That's a positive attitude.

JUAN: I can **move them**, the big ones and the skinny *flaca* ones, the tall ones and the short ones, the good-looking ones and the ugly ones. The smart ones *y estúpido* ones. *Toda la gente.* They just get down when they hear that Chicano music.

EL GATO: Juan, I understand you know Madonna.

....

swap meet street market; neighborhood sale
chump change extra money
silence the critics about make everyone love
move them make everyone dance

JUAN: To be honest, in the music industry you meet all kinds of artists and celebrities.

EL GATO: Is that right? So what's Madonna like?

JUAN: You know, she's kind of like you and kind of like me, and she's sort of like all the people out there in *radiolandia*.

EL GATO: What else? **Fill in the picture.** I'm sure *la gente en radiolandia* want to hear a little *chisme*.

JUAN: *Pues,* I don't know her for real. I mean, I met this dude from a record company who knows this guy who knows this other guy who saw her taking a sip from a soda. *(pause)* The way he described it, it was like I was there for real.

EL GATO: A sip from her soda? You mean you talked to some dude who talked to another dude who talked to another *vato* who saw her **nursing a Big Gulp**?

JUAN: That's it, bro.

EL GATO: I guess I can **picture it**, bro. *(pause)* It's been a while since you had a hit?

JUAN: Nah, last week me and *mis compas* was sitting in the backyard drinking a couple of cold ones—

EL GATO: No, *carnal*! A hit on the radio.

....

Fill in the picture. Tell us more details.
nursing a Big Gulp sipping a drink
picture it imagine it

JUAN: Oh yeah. *Pues,* not since my hit song *"Tort y Frijoles,"* way back in the seventies. Don't you remember the song?

EL GATO: Of course. You sold me a **cassette** at the swap meet.

(JUAN stands up.)

EL GATO: You're gonna do *"Tort y Frijoles,"* that Chicano classic?

(JUAN nods his head.)

EL GATO: Go for it, Juanito! Share it with *la gente!*

JUAN: *(sings with either a raplike beat or the rhythm of a ranchera)*

Tort pushed *Frijoles* on a plate,
Shouting "Take this, take that."
Frijoles, our **piping** brown brother,
Got mad and said, "Meet you outside, homie!
I'm gonna gas you up!"
Tort said, "I'll smear your brown face!"
Frijoles **swung**, *Tortilla* swung—
Frijoles swung two more times
And laid *Tortilla* out flat
With *nalga*-whipping *pleitos*

....

cassette tape recording of the song
Go for it Yes, do it
piping hot; very warm
swung fought

And the slip of a *pedo*.
But *Frijoles* felt sorry for *Tortilla*
Lying in a puddle of guacamole,
And said, "*Tort*, let's go home,
'Cause we go together
Like *chicharrones* and a soda
Like Valenzuela and the Dodgers
Like *menudo* and a *crudo*
Like chips and salsa
Like **mariachis** and a wedding
Like a white T-shirt and khakis
Órale, carnal, we run together
Like *tamales* and Christmas
Like coffee and *chisme*
Like two *vatos* and a Chevy
Like *chorizo y huevos*
Like *pelón y pelón*
Yeah, homes, we run together,
Mano a mano.

(*JUAN returns to sit with EL GATO.*)

EL GATO: That was beautiful, man. Makes me hungry for a little *comida*.

JUAN: I haven't had breakfast myself. In fact, I **skipped**

....

mariachis Mexican musicians
skipped did not eat

dinner last night. Times are tough in Fresno.

EL GATO: I can solve that, Juan. For being on my show, we got two **coupons** for you for dinner at Cuca's Restaurant.

(JUAN takes the coupons and examines them.)

JUAN: I wonder if I can use these for lunch. Dinner ain't for another five hours and my empty stomach is **tripping out with** some weird sounds. I'm hungry now.

EL GATO: Go for it, homes. *(to audience)* Let's give some *aplauso* for Juan-Juan. Catch him at Steaks, Steaks, y Más Steaks. He'll be playing there real soon.

(JUAN strums his guitar. Waves to the audience as lights fade.)

....

coupons sale tickets; free tickets
tripping out with hungry and making

BEFORE YOU MOVE ON...

1. **Paraphrase** Reread pages 17 and 44. Alex and Juan tell Rudy to use his *"boca"* on the date. Tell in your own words what this means.

2. **Foreshadowing** Juan is going to work at Steaks, Steaks, y Más Steaks. Who will he see there? How do you know?

LOOK AHEAD Read pages 59–82. Will Rudy's mother like Patricia?

SCENE FIVE

Mexican American beauty parlor. Rudy's MOTHER is combing her customer ESTELA's hair.

ESTELA: Yeah, the *hombre* was married, and telling me all along that he had to go home to his mother. I should have **had eyes in the back of my head**. No, *tonta* me, I **went along** because of his pretty green eyes and red shoes. He could dance and **talk a story so sweet it gave me goose bumps**. *Pues,* I see him on the street pushing a stroller with a little *mocosa* baby. Then I see his wife, big as a truck—no, bigger, kind of like a couple of big rigs parked together. *(pause as MOTHER combs hair)* Ay, you're pulling my hair!

MOTHER: ¡*Cálmate* Estela! What color do you want your hair this time?

ESTELA: Red.

···

had eyes in the back of my head watched him more closely
went along trusted him
talk a story so sweet it gave me goose bumps tell stories that made me excited and happy

MOTHER: You sure?

ESTELA: *¡Seguro que sí!* **Lent is over** and I can get wild. *(pause)* Do you think redheads have more fun?

MOTHER: *Qué loca*, Estela. Of course not. It's not the color of your hair, it's **your attitude**.

ESTELA: I don't have **an attitude**. My kids got attitudes and my first three husbands had attitudes. But not me. I'm sweet as *flan*. *(stares at mirror, snorting angrily)* Who's that *vieja* staring at me?

MOTHER: Who?

ESTELA: Her!

MOTHER: Her who? What are you talking about?

ESTELA: Her, that ugly *vieja!* I'm going to **scratch her eyes out**!

MOTHER: *(sees that ESTELA is staring at herself in the mirror)* *Loca*, that's you. You're looking in the mirror!

ESTELA: *(laughs)* Oh yeah, I guess it is me. Attractive for her age.

....

Lent is over The religious holiday is finished
your attitude the way you think and feel about things
an attitude a rude way of talking or acting
scratch her eyes out fight her

(pause as MOTHER works on ESTELA's hair)

MOTHER: *Mujer,* when I say "attitude" I'm talking about personality. It doesn't matter what you look like, it's how you are and how you **take each day**.

ESTELA: If that's true, how come you're in the business of making *viejas* like me pretty? Answer that!

MOTHER: Well, perhaps you're right. We all want beauty— and every now and then, to fall in love.

(MOTHER goes to a table, leaving ESTELA making a mean face as she stares in the direction of the mirror. MOTHER returns.)

MOTHER: I have a good husband. He works hard and doesn't **fool around**.

ESTELA: You're lucky, *flaca.* I've been there three . . . no, four times, and I tell you—*bastante!* Men, they're no good! *(pause)* So, your lazy brother finally got a job?

MOTHER: He's playing tomorrow afternoon. *(brightly)* Let's go hear him, give him a little support.

ESTELA: *¡Cómo no!* If your brother wasn't such a lazy bum, I might **hit on him**. *(hears EL GATO's voice)* El Gato's on the radio. Turn it up!

....

take each day respond to what happens each day
fool around date other women; date outside the marriage
hit on him flirt with him; ask him on a date

(MOTHER walks over to the radio and turns up the volume. Lights come up on the suave *EL GATO sitting in the disc jockey's booth.)*

EL GATO: *Buenos días, gente.* I'm coming to you *vivo,* and it's La Love Hour for all of you at work. For those not at work, *pues,* get your *nalgas* down to the unemployment office. Our topic today: love, *amor,* or whatever you want to call it. It's time we talk about man and woman, and the relationships that make us hate life. Ah, just **kidding**. We're here to spin some *discos,* and to answer large, **universal** *cuestiones.* We got someone on the **line stung by Cupid**. *¿Qué pasa?*

CALLER 1: *(offstage)* When is the best time to fall in love, El Gato?

EL GATO: Ahhh . . . when to fall in love . . . *Pues,* I think it's the first of the month, when **the *cheque* comes in**. *(pause)* You're on *la línea.*

CALLER 2: *(offstage)* How do you know love is for real?

EL GATO: Good question! You can tell it's for real if she calls you the next day and remembers your name, not some other dude's. *(pause)* You're on the line.

....

kidding joking
universal common, worldly
line stung by Cupid phone who is in love
the *cheque* comes in you have money

CALLER 3: *(offstage)* Do you always have to close your eyes when you kiss?

EL GATO: Yeah, if you want to pretend it's Jimmy Smits you got in your arms. *(pause)* You're on the line.

CALLER 4: *(offstage)* How can I tell a salad fork from a dinner fork?

EL GATO: Sounds like you just ate at a fancy place. If you're faced with *este problema* in public, forget the forks and *usa una* tortilla. *(pause)* You're on the line.

CALLER 5: *(offstage)* El Gato, I just broke up with my fiancé. Should I return the **engagement ring**?

EL GATO: You know that **pawnshop** on Tulare Street? Just kidding. Yeah, for the sake of karma, mail back the ring. It's probably imitation gold anyhow.

CALLER 6: *(offstage)* I'm thirty-four years old and my *novio* is sixty-six years old. Will it last?

EL GATO: Sure, if he gets **a triple bypass**.

ESTELA: *(gets up from the chair)* *Dáme el teléfono.* I got a question for the *vato.*

....

engagement ring jewelry that showed we were getting married

pawnshop store where you can sell things

a triple bypass heart surgery

EL GATO: Yeah, what is love but some **spring in your legs** and a combination plate from El Pollo Loco? Yeah, love **makes the world spin,** just like *nuestra música. (pause)* Let me get this next one.

(Thirty seconds of music plays.)

ESTELA: El Gato?

EL GATO: You're on the line, baby love.

ESTELA: Yeah. I'm calling to **settle a little debate.**

EL GATO: *¡Adelante!* Go ahead.

ESTELA: *Pues,* I'm over here at House of Beauty and I got to ask, do redheads really have more fun?

EL GATO: Let me **get this straight.** You're asking if the color of your hair improves your sex appeal?

ESTELA: Something like that.

EL GATO: Hair has nothing to do with enjoying life. It's your attitude.

ESTELA: I ain't got an attitude! How come everyone thinks I got an attitude? *¿Por qué?*

....

spring in your legs extra energy
makes the world spin is the most important thing
settle a little debate end a little argument
get this straight understand this

EL GATO: *Fíjate.* I mean the way you are, your calmness, your inner self, *y todo.* You got to learn to **go with the flow**. That you got some smooth-looking hair means nothing. Shoot, I knew a bald woman who **got a kick out of** life more than any *mujer* I ever knew.

ESTELA: *Puro* nonsense.

EL GATO: I'm talking about personality. You got to be nice, not always staring down other *viejas* because your old man looks at another woman. *¿Entiendes?*

(MOTHER nods in agreement.)

EL GATO: And you got to **pick up the dinner tab** now and then, not just expect the dudes to bring out their wallets. You've got to work on your inner self.

(ESTELA hangs up and turns off the radio. EL GATO looks at the telephone and places it back on the receiver. Lights fade from him.)

ESTELA: Inner self. What kind of nonsense is that?

*(MOTHER shrugs her shoulders and puts ESTELA under **an industrial-size** hair dryer. PATRICIA enters and looks around shyly.)*

....

go with the flow relax and have fun
got a kick out of had fun in
pick up the dinner tab pay for dinner
an industrial-size a very large

MOTHER: *Buenos días.* Please come in.

PATRICIA: *Buenos días, señora.*

MOTHER: *Por favor, siéntese.*

PATRICIA: Thank you. *(looks about nervously)* I've never been to a beauty parlor. Most of the time—

MOTHER: I know, your mother cuts your hair.

PATRICIA: Sometimes. Usually my dad does it.

MOTHER: *¿Su papi?* I'm impressed.

PATRICIA: He's got his own **upholstery shop**. He's pretty good **with his hands**.

(pause as MOTHER examines PATRICIA's hair)

MOTHER: You have very fine hair.

PATRICIA: Thank you.

MOTHER: **Glossy** and smooth. No split ends and just a few flakes of **dandruff**.

PATRICIA: I don't do anything special. My mom has nice hair, and I guess I get it from her.

....

upholstery shop store where he covers furniture with fabric
with his hands at building and fixing things
Glossy Shiny
dandruff dry skin

MOTHER: Let me guess. You want your hair curled?

PATRICIA: How did you know?

MOTHER: Instincts. And you're going out on a date? He's a good-looking *muchacho?*

PATRICIA: And sweet.

MOTHER: And you're going to dance the night away?

PATRICIA: Just a lunch date. *(pause)* How tight will you make the curls?

MOTHER: Medium spring. A few precious loops near the back. *(combing PATRICIA's hair)* Is your date—excuse me if I'm direct, *muchacha*—a special person?

PATRICIA: He's a boy from school.

MOTHER: I guess you're **testing the waters**.

PATRICIA: What?

MOTHER: You know, kind of **shopping around**.

ESTELA: Yeah, shopping around. Like going to the Costco of life.

....

Instincts. I guessed because of how I felt.
testing the waters not being too serious about him yet
shopping around seeing if you like him or other boys

PATRICIA: Oh, I guess so. He's just really cute and sweet. I met him when he was working in the cafeteria. He served me an extra **splotch** of chili beans.

MOTHER: Sounds like a **decent** boy.

PATRICIA: I like him because he's honest.

MOTHER: That's good.

PATRICIA: *(looks cautiously at ESTELA, under hair dryer)* But he's younger than me.

ESTELA: I heard that, *muchacha*. Stay away from younger men. They usually have **bad credit**.

MOTHER: *Cállate*, Estela. Let the girl talk. *(to PATRICIA)* So he's younger, and I guess cute because you're pretty yourself.

PATRICIA: *(blushing)* Yeah, he's in ninth grade and I'm in eleventh.

MOTHER: Age is nothing, *m'ija*. It's a modern thing.

PATRICIA: That's exactly what I told my best friend, Alicia. I told her that he has personality, and that's what's important.

....

splotch spoonful
decent nice, sweet
bad credit money problems

MOTHER: That's good.

PATRICIA: He doesn't smoke or **cuss or scrawl** on walls. Rudy's smart, too, for a boy. I even had a dream about Rudy. He was serving me two extra splotches of chili beans.

MOTHER: *(gives PATRICIA a look of surprise)* This Rudy—ah, does he go to Roosevelt High?

PATRICIA: Yeah.

MOTHER: He's kind of small?

PATRICIA: True. He's a little short for his age.

MOTHER: He has a friend named Alex?

PATRICIA: I think so.

MOTHER: And you say he works in the school cafeteria?

PATRICIA: That's right. *(pause)* How do you know all this?

MOTHER: Ah, you know, most kids go to Roosevelt High, and most boys have friends named Alex. Common names and common boys. *(pause)* You're sure about this boy? He *is* younger.

....

cuss or scrawl use bad words or write

ESTELA: *(butting in)* I thought you told this *muchacha* that it's OK to date younger guys.

MOTHER: *(smiles)* I did say that. *(to PATRICIA)* Do you know this boy's family?

PATRICIA: No, except that his mother is overprotective. Kind of **strict**. I mean, he can't go anywhere.

MOTHER: *(bug-eyed, to audience)* Strict! Wait till I speak to that little *mocoso*. I give him ten dollars for his date, and now look at him. **Putting down** his poor mother. *(controls her anger before addressing PATRICIA again)* But his sweet, loving mother must be really nice?

PATRICIA: Actually, he never talks about his mom, aside from her being really strict. I don't know if she's tall or short, or fat or skinny. Young or old. *Nada.*

MOTHER: *(to audience)* See! Already he's forgotten his mommy!

PATRICIA: What?

MOTHER: *(collects herself)* Nothing. *(pause)* So you're in eleventh grade, and I guess you'll be going to college in a couple of years.

....

(butting in) *(interrupting)*
strict serious about rules
Putting down Insulting
(collects herself) *(becomes calm)*

PATRICIA: Maybe. But I thought of joining the **service**.

MOTHER: Don't tell me—the army?

PATRICIA: You're pretty good at **reading my mind**. Yeah, I'd like to travel.

MOTHER: That's good. You should get out of town—I mean, you're young. You should travel. Maybe to Mongolia, or Saudia Arabia, or Timbuktu. Somewhere far, far away.

PATRICIA: Maybe I will. I'll see the world, then come back and marry Rudy. Won't that be something?

MOTHER: *(to audience)* Oh, *m'ijito* is going to get married.

PATRICIA: What?

MOTHER: *(collects herself)* You know, I think all you really need is a blow dry, some shaping here and there, a little off your bangs. But let's get Estela out of the hair dryer.

(MOTHER strolls over to ESTELA. She removes the chrome-colored hair dryer and we discover that ESTELA's hair is bright red.)

ESTELA: *(looking in hand mirror and **primping**)* I like it. I like it a lot. Maybe I do got a attitude after all. *(**shimmies** her hips as lights fade)*

....

service military
reading my mind knowing what I am thinking
primping admiring herself; fixing her hair
shimmies shakes

*RUDY and ALEX are on the front lawn selling apples. They both look **dejected**.*

RUDY: You ever find money on the ground?

ALEX: Just pennies and nickels. *(pause as he reflects)* One time I chased a piece of paper because it looked like a dollar. But it was just a coupon to have your rug **shampooed**.

RUDY: I found a dollar once.

ALEX: Really?

RUDY: Yeah. I spent it on a soda and a box of Cracker Jacks. And guess what I got for my Cracker Jack prize?

(ALEX shrugs his shoulders.)

....

dejected *sad, depressed*
shampooed cleaned

RUDY: A little magnifying glass that I used to burn my *primo's* forehead.

ALEX: No!

RUDY: He was a baby, too.

ALEX: You must have gotten in trouble.

RUDY: *Trouble's* **not the word.** He kept crying, even when I gave him a sip of my soda and let him pull my hair. My mom punished me by making me watch *telenovelas* for two whole weeks. Man, it was **torture**!

ALEX: *(plucks a G.I. Joe from his pocket)* Your left, your left, your left *pata*, your left. Your right, your right, your right *pata*, your right. You think you might join the army?

RUDY: Nah, I don't like uniforms. I don't even like it when my *chones* match my T-shirts. Me, I just throw on anything.

ALEX: I can tell, homes.

RUDY: Clothes are nothing. **It's what's inside that counts.**

ALEX: My cousin Tony's in the marines. He's pretty tough looking. Check this out. When he takes off his shirt, he looks like rocks up and down his stomach.

Trouble's **not the word.** I got punished a lot.

torture horrible

It's what's inside that counts. Your personality is the most important part of you.

RUDY: I want to be like that—tough.

ALEX: I'm hard as a rock.

RUDY: Look more like a fat boulder.

ALEX: Hey, *flaco sapo,* you're always **jumping on my case** just because I put on a little weight. You'll see! Next year I'm going to play **tackle on junior varsity**.

RUDY: Yeah?

ALEX: I'll suit up. I'll put some black stuff under each eye.

RUDY: Shoe polish.

ALEX: Yeah, that stuff. *(dreamily)* I'm going to have my own **rooting section**. They'll be going, "Alex! Alex! Alex!"

RUDY: Who's going to fill your rooting section? You hardly know anyone.

ALEX: What do you mean? In my own family I got three brothers and two sisters. Then there's Mom and Dad, *mis abuelitos, mis primos, mi nina,* and all the rest. We'll **pack the stands**.

RUDY: It'll be like a little Mexico.

....

jumping on my case teasing me
tackle on junior varsity on the football team
rooting section group of people to cheer for me
pack the stands fill the audience

ALEX: That's right.

*(Boys pause as they **munch on** apples.)*

RUDY: We've been out here three hours and not one sale.

ALEX: The economy is down, I guess.

(OLD MAN enters, mumbling to himself. He wanders around the stage before he stops in front of the apple display.)

OLD MAN: Plums?

RUDY: No, they're apples, sir. Five for a dollar. That's twenty cents each.

OLD MAN: You're good at math. What kind of apples are they?

ALEX: Rare antique apples.

OLD MAN: *(repeating slowly)* Rare antique apples.

ALEX: Rare and old.

RUDY: Old as the hills.

OLD MAN: Ah, good in math and a **phrasemaker**. *(examines apples)* Old as the hills, you say.

....

munch on eat
The economy is down People are saving their money
phrasemaker good speaker

RUDY: They might be older than the hills.

ALEX: Old as the seas.

RUDY: The stars.

ALEX: The moon.

RUDY: Mars and Venus.

OLD MAN: And they haven't rotted yet?

RUDY: If you want to know, sir, they're **Garden of Eden apples**.

OLD MAN: **You're pulling my leg!**

ALEX: It's true, sir.

(OLD MAN looks curious.)

RUDY: The red variety is called Eve and the green variety is called Adam.

OLD MAN: You're kidding me.

ALEX: We're talking biblical fruit.

*(With the mention "biblical fruit," OLD MAN **crosses himself**.)*

···

Garden of Eden apples from the special garden that is written about in the Christian Bible

You're pulling my leg! You are lying!

crosses himself *makes a Christian symbol; makes the sign of the cross*

RUDY: That's what my grandmother told us anyway. *(pause)* I bet your wife can make you some empanadas **in a jiffy**.

OLD MAN: *(quietly)* My wife is gone.

ALEX: Shopping?

RUDY: At the beauty parlor?

OLD MAN: **Gone, gone.**

(RUDY and ALEX look at each other, as if to say, How come you opened your big mouth?*)*

OLD MAN: Either of you got a girlfriend?

RUDY: *(eagerly)* **You got someone in mind?**

ALEX: I'm not **picky**. Anyone will do.

RUDY: Yeah, Alex is right. He's not picky. But I sort of have a girlfriend and she's pretty good-looking.

ALEX: *Mentiroso.*

RUDY: You calling Pat ugly?

ALEX: No. You're just going out on a date, that's all. She ain't your girlfriend.

....

in a jiffy very quickly
Gone, gone. She is dead.
You got someone in mind? You know someone I could date?
picky choosy; hard to please

RUDY: She likes me. Doesn't that mean she's my girlfriend?

ALEX: No.

OLD MAN: Boys! Boys! **Put a lid on it.** *(bites into an apple)* I'm seventy-six years old and, well, I haven't gone on a date since my wife passed away three years ago. I haven't done much, actually. To be **frank**, I'm just a boring guy.

RUDY: Don't **put yourself down**. You're really witty. Huh, Alex?

ALEX: Oh yeah.

RUDY: When we first saw you, I thought, *Man, this is a real funny* vato.

OLD MAN: You did?

RUDY: We're Catholic. We wouldn't lie. I thought, *Man, he's **a crackup**.*

OLD MAN: You two boys are OK. But I know I'm boring. I work, I sleep, I eat, I work again.

RUDY: That's more than us. We just eat and sleep.

ALEX: That's right. Just eat and sleep.

....

Put a lid on it. Be quiet.
frank honest
put yourself down say bad things about yourself
a crackup really funny

(OLD MAN still looks sad. RUDY and ALEX huddle together for a brief moment.)

RUDY: Besides selling apples, me and Alex give advice.

OLD MAN: Advice?

RUDY: Personal advice.

ALEX: Advice that would cost thousands **on the open market**.

RUDY: *(in affected voice)* We're part-time romance **specialists**. On slow days we cut lawns and do flower beds.

ALEX: We hardly **charge anything**.

RUDY: We're today's youth. What's the problem, sir?

OLD MAN: This woman I met at bingo . . . Nah, you're too young to understand.

RUDY: Come on, sir. We're nearly fifteen years old. In fact, I have a big date coming up. Older woman.

ALEX: Rudy, I admit, is a little bit older than me, but I've had more experience.

....

on the open market for anyone else
(in affected voice) *(with pride)*
specialists experts
charge anything ask for any money in exchange for advice

RUDY: What do you mean? I've known you since you were, like, in Huggies. You didn't do anything different from me, except almost **flunk** kindergarten because you couldn't figure out your colors.

ALEX: I knew my colors. I just couldn't tie my shoes. *(to OLD MAN)* Yes, I have had a lot more worldly experience.

RUDY: Like what?

ALEX: Things.

RUDY: OK, what kind of things?

ALEX: Well, once I wore a tie.

RUDY: That's it? That's your big "thing"?

ALEX: I wore one to my cousin Bertha's *quinceañera.*

RUDY: A tie ain't nothing. I wore one before. I was **the ring** *vato* in my cousin's cousin's cousin's wedding.

OLD MAN: Put a lid on it, boys. Give me five each.

(ALEX bags the apples and RUDY reflects on the OLD MAN's loneliness.)

....

flunk fail

A tie ain't nothing. Wearing a tie is not special.

the ring *vato* part of the ceremony; the person who carries the ring

RUDY: *(volunteering advice)* Sir, I think you've got to get out.

OLD MAN: Get out?

RUDY: Yeah, you know, go to a movie or a concert or the park or . . . a restaurant.

OLD MAN: A restaurant?

RUDY: Yeah, treat yourself.

OLD MAN: Treat myself, you say? A restaurant. Hmmmm. **Food for thought.**

(OLD MAN reflects on this and leaves stage. ALEX and RUDY sit quietly. RUDY bites into an apple.)

RUDY: Alex, I don't know about girls. They're kind of like high math, hard to figure out.

ALEX: Yeah, I know what you mean. I remember this girl saying that she liked my smile and the next time I saw her, I smiled and she ran away.

RUDY: How come, bro?

ALEX: I had *chicharrones* stuck in my teeth.

....

Yeah, treat yourself. Yes, do nice things for yourself.
Food for thought. I will think about doing that.

RUDY: *(examining ALEX's smile)* I think you got some now, homes.

(ALEX shoves him away and they sit, dejected. Lights fade.)

BEFORE YOU MOVE ON...

1. **Character's Motive** Reread pages 69–71. Why doesn't Rudy's mother tell Patricia that Rudy is her son?

2. **Author's Style** Why did the author add Estela to the play? What is her character's purpose?

LOOK AHEAD Read pages 83–107. Will Rudy's date be a disaster?

SCENE SEVEN

Lights come up on restaurant. A WAITER is setting a table.
WAITER turns when he hears the sound of a guitar playing.
JUAN enters.

JUAN: You won't be disappointed. I'll **wow** the crowd.

(JUAN approaches an empty table and with a pretend microphone
he asks, "What do you think, friend?" He responds for the
*invisible friend, **"Wow."** Repeats this several times, all of the*
invisible couples saying, "Wow.")

JUAN: Yeah, I'm going to wow the place.

WAITER: You don't have to please me. It's the boss. She
expects you to **bring in a crowd**.

(JUAN sits on a stool, places the guitar on his knee, and strums.
*He tunes the guitar. He **eyes** the salsa and chips on a table and*

....

wow impress
"Wow." "Great."
bring in a crowd attract a lot of customers
eyes looks at

begins to help himself. When WAITER returns with flowers for a table, JUAN returns quickly to his stool.)

*(RUDY and PATRICIA walk into the restaurant. RUDY is **awed by the elegance** of the restaurant. With his back to his date, he takes out his wallet and counts his money. He puts the wallet back quickly when he sees the WAITER approaching.)*

WAITER: *(looking up happily)* **Mademoiselle and monsieur.** Please take this seat by the window. *(pulls chair out for PATRICIA)*

PATRICIA: *(sniffs the flower on the table)* It's so romantic. So **sophisticated**, so charming, so . . . And look, a guitarist!

(RUDY sees that it's his UNCLE JUAN, who waves at him. RUDY shakes his head at his UNCLE, as if to say, Don't say anything.)

PATRICIA: It's a discriminating restaurant.

RUDY: Do they discriminate against Latinos? If so, I ain't going to eat here. We'll go grub at Pollo Loco instead.

PATRICIA: No, Rudy. It's just a very fine restaurant. And look, cloth napkins. How fancy!

RUDY: *(studies napkins)* Looks like a diaper.

....

awed by the elegance amazed by the beauty

Mademoiselle and monsieur. Young lady and young man. (in French)

sophisticated fancy, stylish

PATRICIA: Rudy, you're so silly.

(JUAN starts playing his guitar and singing. RUDY and PATRICIA listen. Silly song, perhaps "Tort y Frijoles.")

PATRICIA: He's really talented.

RUDY: He's OK.

WAITER: Our **special for the day** is . . .

(A "mooooo" sounds.)

WAITER: *(continuing)* . . . tender veal. We have spotted cow, brown cow, black-and-white cow, and—

(The mooing sounds again.)

WAITER: I'll be back to get your order. I have to see about something in the kitchen. *(leaves, pulling meat **cleaver** from belt)*

PATRICIA: The food's really . . .

(moo again)

PATRICIA: . . . fresh.

RUDY: Sounds like it's still alive. *(notices her jewelry)* That's a cute cat pin.

....

special for the day food that was specially prepared today
cleaver knife

PATRICIA: I got it when I was eight. That's when we got my cat.

RUDY: What's your cat's name?

PATRICIA: Novio Boy.

RUDY: Novio Boy? You mean, like "sweetheart boy"?

PATRICIA: *(nods her head)* Lots of girl cats find him **adorable**. You want to see a picture of him?

RUDY: Sure.

(PATRICIA pulls a picture from her purse and shows it to him.)

RUDY: And what happened to his ear? It's gone.

PATRICIA: He had a fight with another cat. He's small but he's **valiant**, kind of like you.

RUDY: I'm against fighting.

PATRICIA: That's great!

RUDY: Mostly because when I fight I get beat up.

(RUDY sits and smiles. WAITER approaches.)

WAITER: Have you two decided? The steaks are grade A

---

adorable really cute; handsome
valiant brave

choice, and the hamburger is fresh ground round, premium grade. Of course, you can have chicken. We can fix it up in some enchiladas, *caldo,* or a taco.

RUDY: I'll pass on the *gallina.*

PATRICIA: *(picks up menu)* I'm gonna have the Texas burger with jalapeño cheese. **Jumbo** fries, a chocolate milkshake, a Caesar salad with garlic dressing. And a large homemade root beer.

*(RUDY **grimaces at** the prices on the menu.)*

RUDY: *(muttering to himself)* Four dollars for fries?

PATRICIA: What are you having?

RUDY: I think I'm going to order just a little bit. *(to WAITER)* Crackers and a small diet soda with no ice. I'm wrestling this year and I **have to watch my weight**.

(WAITER writes on his pad and leaves.)

PATRICIA: Same here. I mean, I'm not wrestling, but I have to watch my weight.

RUDY: No way. You look great. *(PATRICIA blushes. Pause.)*

PATRICIA: Guess what?

....

Jumbo An extra big serving of
grimaces at *looks painfully at*
have to watch my weight cannot gain weight

RUDY: You got your driver's permit?

PATRICIA: How did you know? My dad's going to let me start driving next month. Right now he lets me start up the car in the morning.

RUDY: I'm fourteen, and my mom lets me **start up the dryer**. *(pause)* What's your mom like? She nice?

PATRICIA: Tall. Taller than my dad, just about an inch or so. She's pretty nice. But, you know, she's kind of overprotective. She thinks I'm at the library right now.

RUDY: She does?

PATRICIA: She doesn't like me **seeing** boys.

RUDY: Maybe if you told her I'm a freshman it would be all right. If she comes, I can jump in a high chair.

PATRICIA: Maybe, but probably not. She thinks boys are trouble.

RUDY: Am I trouble?

PATRICIA: *(smiling)* 'Course not. As sweet as you are, how could you be trouble? I mean, you're nicer than most boys, and not stupid, either. *(**scoots** her chair closer to RUDY)* I can see that there is something behind your eyes.

....

start up the dryer do the laundry
seeing dating
scoots moves

RUDY: You can?

PATRICIA: Sure. Your eyes . . . they tell me that you're . . . **daring**.

RUDY: Daring?

PATRICIA: Intelligent.

RUDY: Intelligent?

PATRICIA: Loyal.

RUDY: Loyal, too? You can see that in my eyes?

PATRICIA: It's all there.

RUDY: Can you see if I got *ojos mocosos?*

PATRICIA: Rudy, you're silly.

(As they talk, the OLD MAN from the yard sale enters. He looks about as WAITER leads him toward a table. He sees RUDY and stops.)

WAITER: *(leaves)* **Take any seat, sir.**

OLD MAN: *(searching his memory)* Hey, you're that **fella** who sold me the apples, no?

....

daring brave, courageous
Take any seat, sir. Sit at any table, sir.
fella guy

(RUDY, shocked, shakes hands with the OLD MAN.)

RUDY: Yeah, that's me.

OLD MAN: You told me I should treat myself to nice things?

RUDY: *(nervously)* Yeah, that's what I said.

OLD MAN: *(bends down and whispers loudly to RUDY)* She's kind of cute. Do you think you can **fix me up** with her mom?

PATRICIA: Well, actually, my mom is married. *(brightly)* But I'm sure that if she were single, she'd **have her eyes on** someone like you.

OLD MAN: That's good to know. Well, I'm going to have a seat and get a bite to eat. *(loudly, to JUAN)* Say, young man, do you know that one that goes "Ay, ay, ay"?

(RUDY grimaces. OLD MAN finds his seat.)

PATRICIA: How do you know him?

RUDY: Well, he's one of my . . . **clients**.

OLD MAN: *(very loudly)* Those were really good apples that you sold me. The Eve apples were really tasty. *(mumbles and then falls silent)*

---

fix me up get me a date
have her eyes on like; be interested in
clients customers

*(PATRICIA gives a **baffled** look and then stands up when her beeper **goes off**.)*

PATRICIA: My beeper! It's my friend Alicia. Rudy, I'm going to make a call. Be back in a second.

RUDY: Sure.

*(When PATRICIA **is out of earshot**, RUDY speaks to JUAN.)*

RUDY: *Tío*, what are you doing here?

JUAN: It's my new job. What a cosmic coincidence!

RUDY: You're making me nervous.

JUAN: Hey, she's a good-looking girl. A little older.

RUDY: Yeah, older. You ever go out with an older woman, Unc?

JUAN: All the time. And even tall girls. I once went out with a girl with a two-foot vertical jump. Don't **sweat it**, Rudy. *(dips into his pocket for crumpled dollar bills)* Here, dude, this might help out.

RUDY: Thanks, Unc.

....

baffled *confused*
goes off *starts to make noise*
is out of earshot *cannot hear what he is saying*
sweat it *worry*

(JUAN steps forward, stage center.)

JUAN: *(to audience)* Yeah, I've had a few girlfriends hang on my arm. It must have been my Chicano **magnetism**. It sure wasn't my wallet. *(brings out wallet; accordion plastic picture holder falls out)* Yeah, I've lost a lot of them. *(He picks up the folder, and looks at the photos as he **reminisces**.)* There was Teresa, Monica, Laura, Cha-Cha from Dinuba. Then there was Rachel, the violinist. Every time I complained that I didn't have any money, she started pretending to play the violin. And, let's see, there's Veronica and Cindy and Estela and, *híjole*, I forgot all about Gaby, that go-go dancer who danced on TV. *(wiggles his hips)* Then I went out with the twins, Jessica and Jennifer—that was fun, until we played tag-team wrestling and they beat me up. Then there was Lupe and Lupe's cousin, Smiley. *(gives big smile; pause)* I guess I **got around**, and *(looks behind one photo)* mira, I got ten dollars stuck behind Sara! I should have **stuck with** her, my good-luck girl.

(JUAN returns to his stool when PATRICIA returns.)

RUDY: I requested a song for you.

(JUAN begins to sing, "Nothing in my wallet but a little crushed Lifesaver!")

....

magnetism charm, appeal
reminisces remembers
got around had a lot of girlfriends
stuck with kept dating

RUDY: Uncle!—I mean, you! Something quiet.

(JUAN begins to strum a softer, more romantic song.)

(WAITER returns with their order. PATRICIA's eyes widen and RUDY holds up one of his crackers. WAITER leaves after a "bon appétit." PATRICIA cuts the hamburger in two and offers a part to RUDY, who shakes his head.)

PATRICIA: Don't be silly! **Help yourself.** Have some fries. Sounds weird, but I like my fries with mustard.

RUDY: Yeah? Me, too. *(begins to eat PATRICIA's fries)* You ever put potato chips in your sandwich and then smash the sandwich?

PATRICIA: All the time. I like the way it sounds when the chips break up.

(They eat.)

RUDY: *(clearing his throat)* I like your hair. You know, my mom cuts hair for a living.

PATRICIA: Really?

(RUDY pulls a notepad from his pocket and holds it in his lap to read it.)

....

a **"bon appétit"** telling them to have a good meal in French
Help yourself. Have as much food as you would like.

RUDY: Yeah, you have gorgeously mature and exciting hair. Your mouth is big, like a fashion model's mouth. Your eyelashes blow in the wind. You smell good.

(Smiling, RUDY folds the notepad and puts it back into his pocket. PATRICIA smiles at these compliments. They eat silently. ALEX's face appears at the window wearing sun glasses. ALEX enters restaurant, slipping a dollar bill to the WAITER.)

ALEX: A table near those two. *(sits down, then notices the OLD MAN, who is looking at him curiously)*

OLD MAN: Say, you're the one who sold me the apples, no? *(pointing to RUDY)* With your friend there, no?

(ALEX hides behind menu, trying to ignore OLD MAN.)

OLD MAN: Your friend has got a nice girl there . . . Her mom is married. No use in asking.

(PATRICIA gets up and stands by JUAN as he strums the guitar very lightly. She snaps her fingers to the music. RUDY, wiping his mouth, excuses himself to go to ALEX's table.)

RUDY: *(whispering)* ¡Híjole! Pat is **pigging out** and I'm pecking on crackers like a parrot.

ALEX: And the old dude is here.

....

A table near those two. I want to sit next to those two people.

pigging out eating a lot of food

RUDY: He took our advice.

OLD MAN: *(mumbling)* Yeah, you're nice boys. Good advice. Tasty apples! And the girl's mother is married. No use in asking.

(RUDY and ALEX force a smile.)

RUDY: And don't look, but Uncle's playing the guitar. It's his new job.

ALEX: *Your* uncle? Your Tío Juan Juan?

(UNCLE waves to ALEX, who returns his friendly wave.)

ALEX: So how's it going?

RUDY: I don't know. I read from some notes that I wrote down.

ALEX: Forget the notes. **Speak from your heart.** What did you tell her?

RUDY: First I told her I liked her hair.

ALEX: Good.

RUDY: Then I said she has a big mouth, but a good one, a big mouth like a fashion model's.

Speak from your heart. Be honest about your feelings.

ALEX: **Give off** that subject, homes. Talk about her personality. Girls like to hear about stuff like that.

RUDY: *(looks around nervously, then addresses his friend)* Alex.

ALEX: *(mocking)* Rudy.

RUDY: Her mom doesn't know she's with me.

ALEX: So?

RUDY: So, maybe her mom might find out and hit me.

ALEX: That's why you have feet. Run if you see her. **I'll keep an eye out.** *(reaches into his pocket)* Here, man. You can pay me back later.

(ALEX stuffs a wad of money into RUDY's shirt pocket. RUDY smiles and gives his best friend a low five.)

RUDY: You're the best, Alex.

ALEX: OK, get back in there. **Turn on the charm.** Don't worry about her mom. *(pause)* But if her dad shows up, then you run. I got my bike outside.

(RUDY, straightening the collar of his shirt, returns to the table; PATRICIA hurries to the table as well.)

·······································

Give off Stop talking about

I'll keep an eye out. I will watch to see if Patricia's mom comes here.

Turn on the charm. Be interesting and cute.

PATRICIA: Is he a friend of yours?

RUDY: Kind of. *(pause)* Patricia, you got a . . . **complex** personality. I mean, you're not stuck-up. You're willing to go out with a boy who . . .

PATRICIA: What?

RUDY: *(shyly)* Never mind.

PATRICIA: Come on, tell me.

RUDY: Who still has his G.I. Joes.

PATRICIA: You're cute! *(pause)* You know, I saw you play baseball before.

(RUDY perks up.)

PATRICIA: You were at the playground.

RUDY: Was I any good?

PATRICIA: No, but I liked how you tried really hard.

RUDY: Well, I like baseball. It just feels good, standing in the box when the outfielders are playing in. You got to **grip the bat like you mean it**, kick at the dirt in the batting box, stare at the pitcher like you hate him, and do this.

....

complex mysterious; difficult to understand
grip the bat like you mean it hold the bat tightly

(spitting into palms) And before, at home, you got to iron your jersey, put some black shine under your eyes, polish your mitt, and put on . . . *(becomes shy)*

PATRICIA: What?

RUDY: It's something private. *(scribbles a note and hands it to PATRICIA)*

PATRICIA: Oh, your athletic supporter.

RUDY: Last year I was wearing size Small, but I'm up to Medium now. *(smiles proudly to himself)*

*(Rudy's MOTHER and her friend ESTELA enter the restaurant. **Each recognition that follows should be individually and sequentially highlighted.** The MOTHER immediately sees RUDY, but he doesn't see her. ESTELA points at the young couple—RUDY and PATRICIA—the MOTHER shushes ESTELA. ALEX sees Rudy's MOTHER; ALEX gulps and hides behind a menu. JUAN raises a finger to his mouth. The two women take seats quietly and hide behind menus.)*

(WAITER enters and takes away RUDY's and PATRICIA's plates and gives them a menu.)

(RUDY and PATRICIA look at each other. RUDY takes the

....

Each recognition that follows should be individually and sequentially highlighted. *The characters should look at each other one at a time and in order.*

menu and opens it up.)

WAITER: *(to his new customers)* I'll be with you in a moment.

RUDY: If you want, you can have dessert.

PATRICIA: No, I'm fine. That was good.

RUDY: *(continuing romantically)* Pat, I like your hair.

PATRICIA: Thanks. I had it blow-dried.

RUDY: *(pulls his notepad from his pocket and reads from it surreptitiously)* You **exude cool vibrations** that make me feel like a—*(deep voice)* like a man. *(back to regular voice)* You remind me of a crashing ocean, my **mermaid**. Or flowers in spring.

MOTHER: *¿Qué?* "My mermaid"?

(RUDY looks around the restaurant; his MOTHER raises menu to her face. RUDY continues reading.)

RUDY: You're the scent of spring—

MOTHER: Scent of spring!

RUDY: *(looks around again)* Your hands are like doves—

....

surreptitiously *secretly, sneakily*
exude cool vibrations communicate in sweet ways
mermaid beautiful sea creature

ESTELA: *¡Qué romántico!*

RUDY: *(looks in direction of the women)* Excuse me, Pat. *(RUDY gets up and looks behind the menu. He is shocked but quickly **recovers**. He starts to walk back to his table.)*

OLD MAN: *(loudly whispers)* Hey. *(RUDY stops near OLD MAN.)*

OLD MAN: Say, you know those women who just came in?

RUDY: Not really.

OLD MAN: *(in loud whisper)* The redhead is kind of cute. Go ask if she's married.

RUDY: I can't do that!

OLD MAN: What, you scared of work? I'll give you two dollars.

RUDY: *(still feeling **short of money**, agrees. He goes up to ESTELA.)* That gentleman asked about you. *(ESTELA looks over at the OLD MAN and waves flirtatiously. RUDY returns to his table.)*

PATRICIA: Do you know them?

RUDY: *(nervously)* No, I never saw them before.

....

recovers *acts as if nothing is wrong*
short of money *like he does not have enough money*

(JUAN strums dance music.)

PATRICIA: Let's dance, Rudy.

RUDY: Dance? No, I'm too full. Those crackers filled me up.

PATRICIA: Come on, Novio Boy. No one's around, except your friend.

*(PATRICIA lifts RUDY from the chair and pulls him almost roughly. PATRICIA tries to dance closely but RUDY struggles to dance **at arm's length, conscious of his mother's watching**. They dance until WAITER coughs for their attention and approaches.)*

WAITER: Your bill, *monsieur*.

RUDY: Thank you. (**gulps** *as he reads the bill. He digs into his pocket.)*

PATRICIA: We can **split this**.

RUDY: No, I got it. What's twenty-four dollars and fifty-four cents to me?

PATRICIA: Next time, it's my turn. Oh, wait! I'll pay the tip!

RUDY: OK.

....

at arm's length, conscious of his mother's watching *far away from Patricia because he knows his mother is watching*

gulps *swallows loudly as if upset*

split this both pay for part of this

PATRICIA: I have to be home by two o'clock. I had a lot of fun, Rudy.

RUDY: Me, too. *(pause)* You don't mind if I'm younger?

PATRICIA: Of course not. *(pause)* Listen, I'll teach you how to drive a car.

MOTHER: Drive a car!

PATRICIA: *(looks toward the women)* Are those women talking to us?

RUDY: Nah, they're just **chattering**.

PATRICIA: So—you want to learn? We can practice going back and forth in the driveway.

RUDY: *¡Simón!* And I got my license, too.

PATRICIA: You do?

RUDY: Well, it's not a real license. It's a license on my bike that says RUDY. It hangs behind my seat.

PATRICIA: *(laughs)* You're a fun date. And a good dancer.

(PATRICIA gives RUDY a kiss on his cheek. She leaves.

....

chattering talking to each other

RUDY looks at his MOTHER and ESTELA angrily as they slowly lower the menus from their faces.)

RUDY: How come you're **spying on me**?

MOTHER: I'm not, *m'ijo*! Me and Estela came here to hear your uncle.

(JUAN strums guitar.)

MOTHER: I didn't know this is where you were taking your date.

RUDY: You're **snooping**! I know you are!

MOTHER: Cross my heart. I didn't know, really.

ESTELA: *(to Rudy's MOTHER)* She's the girl whose hair you cut yesterday, *qué no?*

RUDY: You did her hair, Mom? She knows you?

MOTHER: *(angry)* What, are you embarrassed? Ashamed of your mommy?

RUDY: No, it's just that . . . Mom, I can't get any privacy! You're here, Estela is here, and Alex, and Uncle! And even the guy we sold apples to. Everyone!

....

spying on me following and watching me
snooping trying to learn about my date

JUAN: *(to RUDY)* Rudy, it's a cosmic thing that we gathered around you. We're **watching out for** you. *(to MOTHER)* But we got to give him **a little space**, *hermana*.

*(**Bug-eyed**, they all stare at RUDY)*

RUDY: Well, you're doing too much watching.

MOTHER: She's a nice girl.

ESTELA: Pretty, *también*.

RUDY: You like her?

MOTHER: She's a good girl. But I don't want you driving a car with her. *(pinching his cheek)* My little boy is growing up.

(ESTELA eyes the OLD MAN, who has gotten up and joined them.)

OLD MAN: Say, I like your hair.

ESTELA: Thank you.

OLD MAN: And your smile.

ESTELA: That's sweet.

OLD MAN: And you possess an attitude that—

....

watching out for protecting
a little space some privacy
Bug-eyed *Looking surprised*

ESTELA: *(angrily)* Why does everyone think I got an attitude?

OLD MAN: A nice attitude. *(pause)* You married?

ESTELA: *(flirting)* Sometimes.

*(OLD MAN smiles, then **is at a loss as to** how to continue.)*

OLD MAN: *(whispering to RUDY)* What should I do next?

RUDY: Maybe you should take them on a walk or something. And don't forget to get her number.

OLD MAN: You gals care to go for a walk? And can I get your telephone number?

(OLD MAN, Rudy's MOTHER, and ESTELA leave the restaurant. JUAN, RUDY, and ALEX sit down at their table.)

ALEX: *Mira,* she left a french fry. Here, Novio Boy. *(feeds it to RUDY)*

RUDY: She wiped me out for the rest of ninth grade. But it **beats** doing nothing.

(At this JUAN begins to play his earlier song about "nothing" from Scene 3.)

RUDY: Thanks for helping out, Unc.

....

is at a loss as to *does not know*
beats is better than

JUAN: *No problema.* You're my only nephew. About the money . . . You can pay me back later.

ALEX: But me first.

(JUAN returns to his stool and starts strumming his guitar softly.)

RUDY: I'm gonna have a yard sale, so I can earn back what I owe you and Mom and Uncle.

ALEX: What are you gonna sell?

RUDY: My G.I. Joes. And my baseball cards. And my basketball and my Ninja Turtle lunch box.

ALEX: Not your Ninja Turtle lunch box!

RUDY: This is a clearance sale! *¡La gran pulga!* Out with it all!

ALEX: I'll help you out. I got some stuff underneath my bed. We'll have *una gran* swap meet right on the front lawn.

RUDY: You'll do that for me?

ALEX: *Simón,* bro. We ninth graders **got to stick together**.

RUDY: Like *tortillas y frijoles.*

....

This is a clearance sale! I will sell everything for very low prices!

got to stick together need to help each other

ALEX: Guacamole *y* chips!

RUDY: *¡Huevos con chorizo!*

ALEX: Soda *y* sunflower seeds!

*(They shake hands **elaborately**.)*

RUDY: You're the best, homes.

ALEX: Man, it's tough being a Novio Boy.

....

elaborately with pride; with feeling

BEFORE YOU MOVE ON...

1. **Cause and Effect** Rudy's family and friends are at the restaurant during Rudy's date. How does this affect him?

2. **Conclusions** Reread pages 105–107. Why does everyone call Rudy "Novio Boy" at the end of the play?

SPANISH WORDS AND PHRASES

abuelita/o	grandmother/grandfather
¡Adelante!	Go forward!
amor	love
aplauso	applause
asco	sickening, nauseated feeling
ay, dios	oh, god
ay, este malo chavalo	oh, this bad boy
bastante	enough
boca	mouth
borracho	drunkard
buena suerte	good luck
buenos días	good day; hello
caldo	soup
¡Cállate!	Be quiet, shut up!
¡Cálmate!	Calm down!
carnal	buddy
chola	tough girl
chale	no way
chavalo	kid
cheque	check
chicas	girls
chicharrones	fried pork rinds
¡Chihuahua!	Hey! Wow!
chisme	gossip
chones	underwear
chorizo	sausage
claro que sí	of course
coche	car
cochino	dirty, piglike

comida	food
¿Cómo no?	of course
cosa	thing
crudo	hung over; a hangover
cuando quieran	whenever they want
cuestiones	questions
curandera	healer, witch
Dáme el teléfono	Give me the phone
dedica (dedicatoria)	dedication
de veras	really, truthfully
discos	records
empanada	pastry turnover
en serio	seriously
¿Entiendes?	(Do you) understand?
Es mi favorito, también	It's my favorite, too
escuincle	little kid
ese	guy
¡Espérate!	Wait!
este problema	this problem
estúpida/o	stupid
Fíjate	Pay attention
flaca/o	skinny girl/boy
flan	custard
frijoles	beans
fuchi	smelly
fuerte	strong
gallina	hen
gallo	rooster

gente	people
gran pulga	big swap meet
guitarra	guitar
guitarrista del valle	guitarist from the valley
hermana/o	sister/brother
híjole	wow
hombre	man
huango	stretched out
huevo	egg
huevos con weenies	eggs scrambled with frankfurters
interesante	interesting
jefe	chief, boss
jeta	pout
la línea	the line
lágrimas	tears
loca/o	crazy
lo mejor	the best
malo	bad
mano a mano	hand in hand
más	more
mentirosa/o	liar
menudo	tripe soup
m'ija/o	my daughter/son
m'ijita/o	my little daughter/son
mi/s	my
¡Mira!	Look!
mis compas (compadres)	my buddies
mocosa/o	snotty kid

muchacha/o	girl/boy
muchísimas gracias	thank you very very much
mujer	woman
la música a la gente	the music to the people
muy	very
muy fuerte y bravo	very strong and brave
nada	nothing
nalgas	buttocks
nina	godmother
novia/o	sweetheart
no problema	no problem
No te preocupes	Don't worry
nuestra música	our music
ojos mocosos	mucus in the eyes
órale	all right
pan dulce	sweet bread, pastry
papi	daddy
pata	foot
pedo	fart
pelón	bald man
pero	but
placas	graffiti signatures
pleitos	fighting
por favor	please
¿Por qué?	Why?
prima/o	cousin
pues	well, uh
pulga	swap meet
puro	pure

¿Qué?	What?
qué loca	how crazy
¿Qué no?	Right? Isn't that so?
¿Qué pasa?	What's going on?
¿Que romántico!	How romantic!
¿Quién es esta muchacha?	Who's this girl?
quinceañera	party celebrating a girl's fifteenth birthday
radiolandia	radio land
ranchera	old-fashioned love song
raza	the Latino people
sapo	chump
secreto	secret
seguro que sí	of course, certainly
señor/a	Mr./Mrs.
Siéntese	Sit down
simón	yes (emphatic)
Soy un poeta de Aztlán	I'm a poet from Aztlán
su	your
también	also
telenovelas	television soap operas
tío/a	uncle/aunt
toda la gente	all the people
toda/o	all of it/everything/everybody
tonta/o	stupid
tu	your
un momento	just a minute
una	one, a
usa	use

valle	valley
vato	guy
veinte dólares	twenty dollars
vieja/o	old woman/man
Viva la raza	Long live our people
vivo	live, alive
y	and
y todo	and all the rest
Uncle Juan's song:	

No menudo en mi bowl	No soup in my bowl
y nada en mi estómago.	and nothing in my stomach.
¡Nada, nada, nadaaaaa!	Nothing, nothing, nothing!